POCKET IMAGES

Blaina, Nantyglo and Brynmawr

Dunlop Semtex Ltd, Brynmawr, c.1957, showing the manufacture of carpet cushioning. Calendered rubber and hessian is being fed into a vulcaniser. Paddy O'Keefe stands first left.

POCKET IMAGES

Blaina, Nantyglo and Brynmawr

Trevor Rowson

Edited by Simon Eckley

NONSUCH

Boys on Forge Rise, Nantyglo, c.1900.

This book is dedicated to my grandson, James Rowson.

First published 1995
This new pocket edition 2006
Images unchanged from first edition

Nonsuch Publishing Limited
The Mill, Brimscombe Port,
Stroud, Gloucestershire, GL5 2QG
www.nonsuch-publishing.com

Nonsuch Publishing Ltd is an imprint of Tempus Publishing Group

The right of Trevor Rowson and Simon Eckley to be identified as the Authors
of this work has been asserted in accordance with the
Copyrights, Designs and Patents Act 1988.

British Library Cataloguing in Publication Data.
A catalogue record for this book is available from the British Library.

ISBN 1-84588-253-9

Typesetting and origination by Nonsuch Publishing Limited
Printed in Great Britain by Oaklands Book Services Limited

Contents

Brynmawr Square, c.1950. Notice the bus ready to depart for Abergavenny.

Foreword

The Ebbw Fach valley has always engendered great feelings of affection and local pride in its natives and, over the centuries, it has been well served by its local historians. As long ago as 1779, Edmund Jones (who was born at Pen Llwyn on the hill above Roundhouse Farm) was moved to write that this parish:

> "is an instance where the agencies of god upon the Land and upon and among the Inhabitants have been so remarkable and such things have come to pass in it in the course of time, the like whereof, it may be, cannot be showed out of any other Parish in the Kingdom; . . . 'tis pity the knowledge of them should be retained from the publick."

Trevor Rowson has an honoured place in the long tradition of local history in this valley. Over more than forty years, he has striven to ensure that the "things that have come to pass in it" will never be retained from the publick". His enthusiasm, commitment and sheer depth of knowledge have been an example and inspiration to other local historians, professional and amateur alike. I consider it a very great honour to be asked to contribute a foreword to this remarkable book.

Frank Olding
Curator
Abergavenny Museum

Introduction

The area covered by this book stands at the head of the Ebbw Fach river, extending from Blaina in the south to Brynmawr in the north. Hills rise steeply on either side of the valley in places to over 1,500 feet. The three communities of Blaina, Nantyglo and Brynmawr project themselves against a strong Welsh background and local histories have repeatedly told of their customs, romantic legends, passion for education, quick wit and considerable contribution to culture in our country of music and song.

The history of the area during the last two centuries has been dominated, however, by the growth and subsequent decline of the iron and coal industries and the dramatic social and economic consequences of this rise and fall, which continue to be felt today. Because of the almost insatiable demand for the iron and coal produced in the area, new and vibrant communities grew up through the nineteenth century in what was hitherto a largely unpopulated region of south Wales. By 1800 the greatest upheaval in the area's history was well underway. Yet only a few decades earlier the area was unspoiled: milkwort and harebell covered the gentle slopes of the Milfraen mountain, red kite flew silently and swiftly on the breeze, while below the Ebbw river, teaming with trout, meandered through the wooded valley. However, beneath the surface of the land lay the timebomb of substantial mineral wealth awaiting exploitation. With the advent of industrialisation, sulphurous smoke made the daytime sky yellow and the nights red. The sound of sweating workers and beasts of burden mingled with the clatter of drams carrying raw materials to feed the furnaces.

In 1795 the first ironworks in Nantyglo was opened by Harford, Hill and Co. It comprised of two furnaces, several forges, a steam engine and other buildings and machinery necessary for the smelting and forging of iron. The first workers' houses were built in Market Road and were known as the Long Row. They were constructed against a rock ledge forming two tenements one above the other. However, in 1796 the works closed due to continued dispute over investment, and they remained closed until 1802 when they were purchased by Joseph Harrison. Yet Harrison, too, had insufficient financial backing and the works were not re-opened for long. It was not until 1811, when Joseph Bailey together with Matthew Wayne came to Nantyglo and bought the Works for £8,000, that a period of sustained development was able to begin. In 1820 Wayne retired from the Works and his place was taken by Crawshay Bailey, brother of Joseph. By 1825 as the pace of industrialisation quickened, there were seven blast furnaces at Nantyglo, 500 houses on 5,000 acres of surface property, eleven seams of coal were worked above and below ground, and an estimated 150 miles of tramroad had been laid. In total, the Baileys then employed 3,000 men and 500 women and children. In 1844 the famous Lion Mill was opened consolidating Nantyglo's position as one of the most important iron-producing centres in the world.

Earlier, about 1820, the Baileys had turned their attention to the construction of a personal residence, Tŷ Mawr or Nantyglo House, which would reflect their burgeoning wealth and dominance of the local community. This mansion contrasted greatly with the miserable dwellings lived in by the ironworkers and colliers. Compelled to adhere to the truck system and buy only from the company shop most workers were at this time, before legislation began to ease their conditions, virtual slaves of the ironmasters working long shifts at the works or mines and seeing precious little daylight during the winter months.

However, because of these harsh and brutal conditions, violent protest was never far from erupting from beneath the surface. Riots and disturbances were quite common and such was the resentment felt against Crawshay Bailey that he feared for his life and built, for his own protection, two fortified towers – the Nantyglo Roundhouses. Cyclical slumps in the demand for iron, allied with falling wages and rising bread prices, often produced a mood of militancy in Nantyglo. The area was roamed by bands of men with blackened faces and wearing animal skins, men known as the Scotch Cattle who tried to enforce the acceptance of trade unions and who attacked any workers who opposed their ideas. In 1822 a "combination" of Nantyglo workers led by Josiah Evans and Harry Lewis defeated local militiamen and reinforcements had to be summoned to restore order. For almost a fortnight the Scots Grays were billeted in the stables of the Roundhouse complex.

By the late 1830s a new protest organisation had emerged in Chartism and one of the movement's leading figures in South Wales was Zephaniah Williams, landlord at the Royal Oak Inn in Queen Street, Nantyglo. The local ironmasters and clergy organised anti-Chartist meetings and, at Coalbrookvale House, Crawshay Bailey made an impassioned speech in defence of the status quo and attacking Chartism. "I owe all that I have to my own industry…", he stated defiantly if somewhat deceitfully, "and I would risk my life rather than lose my property." However, it was at Nantyglo, outside the Royal Oak, that the Heads of the Valleys column of Chartists led by Williams gathered on 3 November 1839 for the march on Newport. The following morning the Chartists stormed the Westgate Hotel seemingly unaware that well-armed soldiers were stationed inside the building. Volleys of shots were fired into the crowd killing 22 and wounding 50 more. Among the dead were Abraham Thomas, Isaac Thomas and Jon Jonathan, all from Nantyglo. The ringleaders of the rising were arrested by the authorities and charged with high treason. On 2 February 1840, his death sentence commuted to transportation for life, Zephaniah Williams, together with John Frost and William Jones (Chartist leader from Pontypool), set sail for Australia. He was never to see his native land again and died in Launceston, Tasmania in 1874.

Today, many acres of the land damaged by the iron industry and mining have been reclaimed for the use of the present inhabitants of Blaina, Nantyglo and Brynmawr. The slag and coal tips and the tiny workers' houses clinging to the hillside have become part of the past of our community. It is hoped, therefore, that this book will help stimulate the memories of its readers and show this, and future generations how we lived, worked and played, and the way things were.

Trevor Rowson

St Anne's church, young wives and mothers, 1950. Among those pictured are Mrs Wheeler, Mrs Sims, Mrs Wellington, Mrs Bull, Mrs Williams, Mrs Williams "Cawl".

One

Iron and Coal

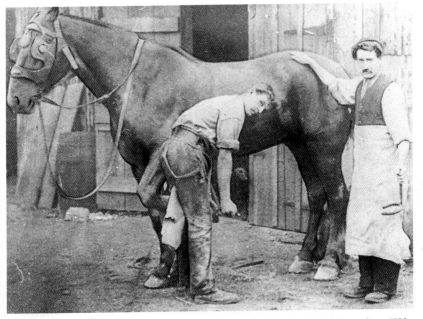

Fred Price (right), blacksmith at the Blaina Ironworks, outside the stables with his boy striker, c.1920.

Crawshay Bailey, the Nantyglo ironmaster, at Newport Docks in 1867, viewing the clipper ship named after him. On its maiden voyage the vessel took part in the Great China Tea Run during which it ran into a typhoon and, despite losing most of its cargo and one of its masts, managed to survive. However, the clipper's luck was not to hold for, in 1869, it set sail for America and was never seen or heard of again. The Nantyglo Ironworks had been bought in 1811 by Joseph Bailey. Later, Crawshay Bailey joined his brother and they controlled the works together until Joseph's retirement in 1833. The works flourished for many decades but by the 1870s, by which time Crawshay Bailey had retired to Llanfoist where he died in 1872, the iron industry in South Wales, increasingly being superceded by steel production, was already in terminal decline, often hastened by bad management. Bailey, however, did not live to see the collapse of the fountain of his wealth as the works clung on until dismantling began in 1878.

The Roundhouses, Nantyglo. In 1816 a slump in demand for iron, due to the end of the Napoleonic Wars coupled with horrendous working conditions, had led to a rapid deterioration in labour relations. Crawshay Bailey so feared for his life when riots broke out amongst his workers that he had two fortified towers built as a protection against the militancy of his men. They were the last castle-type fortifications to be built in Britain.

Nantyglo Ironworks and workers' housing. In the centre are the forges and rolling mills. In the background is Cwm Crachen valley with above, Blaen-nant Farm and the Cornish Pit.

Blaina Ironworks was opened in 1823 by George Jones and John Barker. Later, the works was sold on to Messrs Thomas Brown and John Russell of Risca who ran the works until 1846. From then until its closure in 1878 the works was owned by Frederick Levick and

John Simpson. Later, the site was re-opened as a tinworks and continued in business until 1906. Visible, to the right of the picture, are the Lamb Inn and Inkerman Row, and, in the foreground, the coking ovens.

The disused limekilns from Nantyglo Ironworks. In 1885 a couple set up home in one of the kilns and raised three children there. In 1906, following a public outcry, they were moved out.

Henwain pit, Blaina, 1880s. Many of the local pits were flooded during the three month strike of 1880 after pumping had been disrupted. However, by the following year production had returned to normal with 861,904 tons of coal leaving Blaina pits for the docks at Newport.

General view of Nantyglo, c. 1910. Under the embankment to the left were the coal levels owned by Mr Ted Rowe. To the right is the Boot Inn, Boot Row (now Beaumont Close) with the Golden Lion public house behind. Above these is Coedcae – now the site of a large housing estate.

Colliers working in a level at Blaen-nant in 1913. Notice the candles on the floor which were at that time the main source of illumination for the men. Mr Ben Francis worked in these levels for twenty-five years using candles as the means of lighting. One day he was loaned a carbon lamp and described the experience thus: "Duw, boy, it was like working in daylight!"

Stone's Colliery, opened 1860 and closed in 1918. It had many different names during its lifetime – in 1873, under the ownership of the Nantyglo and Blaina Co. Ltd, it was known as the Rising Sun Colliery. By 1877 Morgan & Williams were the owners and they named it the Sun Pit. Two years later it was known as the Sun Pit Old and New by its new proprietors, Stone Bros. Thereafter, it was owned by J.W. Stone who called it the New Sun Pit and then the North Blaina pit.

The Lower Deep Colliery. Owned by John Lancaster & Co. Ltd this pit opened in 1860. In 1893 the Old Coal Vein was abandoned and the pit finally closed in 1922 although it was maintained as a pumping station for some years after.

Silvanus Jones & Co. screens, Nantyglo, c.1919. This company was founded in 1820 and was subsequently run by three generations of Silvanus Jones – grandfather, father and son. The site is now covered by the playing fields of Nantyglo Comprehensive School.

South Griffin Colliery, Blaina, c.1914. Owned by the Lancaster Company it was closed in 1921.

Trucks of coal leaving Blaina for the docks at Newport. Blaina Tinworks stands on the left.

Above: Inside a coal level high up on the mountainside above Cwm Celyn, 1920s. On the left is Mr Davies and on the right Mr Charlie Pugh. This level was later taken over by the Davies family of Blaina. As in many levels rising water proved a considerable problem here and on one occasion a trapped pony was drowned.

Right: A tramline running down the hillside from the coal level at Cwm Celyn. Visible on the right is Tyn-y-Ffald Farm and, in the distance, Yellow Row.

Above: One of the Quakers' levels at Coalbrookvale, 1930s, on the former site of the Coalbrookvale furnaces – in the background is the house built for the ironmaster George Brewer in the 1830s.

Opposite: The levels at Coalbrookvale, 1931. These had been opened by the Quakers to ease unemployment in the area. In 1930, in Brynmawr, unemployment among insured males was as high as 90 per cent and with Nantyglo and Blaina also suffering from chronic shortage of work the area was perhaps the blackest spot in South Wales during the Depression. Such a bleak situation led inevitably to the forced migration of many thousands of men in search of work in the more prosperous areas of Britain, particularly the south-east of England. However, the population refused to accept their plight and when the indifference of London to the poverty and suffering of South Wales was expressed in the harsh measures of the Unemployment Assistance Board Act of 1934-35 they reacted with justifiable violence. On 3 February 1935 tens of thousands of people throughout South Wales rose up in defiance of the means test, and the system which lay behind it, in the largest mass demonstration the Welsh nation had ever seen (an estimated total of 300,000 men, women and children participated altogether). In the Ebbw Fach valley, where a strong Communist presence had seen the election of district and county councillors from the party, protest was particularly widespread leading to bitter clashes with the police and several arrests. Communist councillor, Phil Abrahams was subsequently stripped of his civil rights for ten years for his involvement in the disturbances and other men were jailed for several months.

Left: Mrs Staley and friend, Church Street, Blaina, 1930s, with the remains of the Lower Deep Colliery in the background. All the houses have now disappeared.

Right: Three miners on Forge Rise in the 1930s. The now demolished Welsh Wesleyan Chapel can be seen in the background.

Beynon's Colliery, 1930s. This was sunk in the early 1920s to alleviate the unemployment problems in Blaina after the closure in 1921 of the South Griffin Colliery. It initially employed 500 men. It was the last working mine in the upper Ebbw Fach valley until its demolition began in 1976.

Mr Alf Davies, pictured outside Beynon's Colliery, 1940s.

Two

Transport

Black Rock Limekilns, 1909. These were built in the early nineteenth century to supply both the Clydach Ironworks and local agriculture.

An early Griffin bus, Notice the canvas roof and the solid spoked wheels. The company had been started by local entrepreneur, Tom Jones who ran the first bus service between Brynmawr and Blackwood. He took over the Griffin Mews for his garage and called his buses the Griffin service. One of his first vehicles was an army surplus lorry onto the chassis of which was fitted a small bus body.

Clydach Gorge, 1920s. On the right is the railway opened in 1862 to replace Crawshay Bailey's tramroad of 1822. The supports for the tramroad (on the left) were built by Thomas Danford in 1795 and can still be seen today.

Nantyglo railway station. The line between Nantyglo and Blaina was known as "the missing link" as the two towns were not connected until 1905. By 1862 a railway line had been opened from Merthyr to Abergavenny through Brynmawr. There was soon a clamour for a connection to be built with the GWR line which terminated at Nantyglo. However, several decades passed, during which time the journey between Nantyglo and Brynmawr had to be completed in horse-drawn vehicles, before a rail link was completed. It was opened with great ceremony on 12 July 1905 by the Duke and Duchess of Beaufort.

A canvas-topped bus struggles its way up the Black Rock at Brynmawr in the 1930s. This stretch of road was also known as Joby's Pitch after one Joby Davies who, from the 1920s, ran a slaughterhouse under the arches there.

The aftermath of a train derailment near the Tiler's Arms, Blaina, 1934.

Mr Raymond Huggins standing proudly next to his Austin car, c.1935.

Above: Mr Trapnell of Blaina delivering milk on Farm Road, Nantyglo, 1940s.

Right: The new road being laid at Twyn-y-Deryn following the 1947 explosion which destroyed the old Porter's road. The building in the centre is the Pentecostal chapel.

Embassy bus, Brynmawr, late 1940s.

Looking south along High Street, Blaina, with the old entrance to Beynon's Pit on the right.

The old railway lines, Nantyglo which were dismantled in 1963. On the right is Market Road and the old company shop from the Nantyglo Ironworks. The chimney in the background belongs to the slag-crushing plant opened in 1919 to produce hard-core for roads and house construction.

The Brecon and Monmouthshire Canal and the warehouse at Govilon. Iron from the Nantyglo Iron works was brought here to be loaded onto barges.

Three

Trade and Industry

Bush Inn, High Street, Blaina, c.1910.

Jack Lewis in front of his newspaper shop, Garnfach, 1930s. The previous owner's name can still be seen above the window.

Boot-making at a Quaker factory in Brynmawr, 1930s. Brynmawr Bootmakers Ltd was established by the Society of Friends in 1929 to produce heavy footwear for miners and agricultural workers, miners safety boots and cycling shoes. It operated first from premises on Factory Road moving in 1937 to Warwick Road and later to a brand new factory beside Winchestown Road, Nantyglo. The area was greatly helped during the Depression by the Coalfields Distress Committee of the Society of Friends and later by the Mansion House Fund. Both tried hard to diversify economic activity by promoting the development of light industry as a source of employment for the many unable to find work in the declining mining sector and its subsidiary industries.

A boy, one of many who, a generation before, would have followed their fathers down the pit, learning how to make tweed, c.1934.

Billy Jones of Twyn-y-Deryn (left) and Raymond Huggins delivering goods to customers in Gwent Terrace, c.1938.

Mr Huggins (left) at his grocery shop in Queen Street with son Raymond and assistants Pat Griffiths and Betty Davies, c.1956. The shop opened in 1932 and closed in 1969.

Mr Trapnell delivering milk with motorbike and sidecar, Farm Road, Nantyglo, 1940s.

Aerial view of the Waun Pond, Dunlop Semtex and Brynmawr, *c.*1962. On the far right are the sidings at Brynmawr railway station and behind the factory complex St Ann's Church nestles among the trees. After much lobbying notably by the leading Quaker, Lord Jim Forrester, the Dunlop Semtex factory was constructed between 1948 and 1950. Producing a wide variety of industrial goods, it considerably alleviated the deep-seated unemployment problem in the area. Its innovative design, apparently based on the Festival Hall in London, led to it being declared a listed building after its closure in 1981.

Above: Workers from the engineering department at Dunlop Semtex, 1960s. Among those pictured are David Brown, Don Phillips, David Morgan, Len Langdon, Arthur Phillips, Barry Davies, Wyndham Kershaw, Charlie Roberts and Mr Tucker.

Left: Woman workers in 1961 outside the factory of Dannimac Ltd, makers of quality raincoats. From left to right: Masie James, May Davies, Iris Thomas, Ann Morris, Mima Roberts, Carol Dobbins, Elsie Masey. The siting of the Dannimac factory at Brynmawr brought new employment opportunities into the area although, in a pattern repeated through the valleys of South Wales in the post-coal era, the new jobs were principally for women workers.

Cooper's Factory, Nantyglo, 1970s. Among those pictured are Val Hardacre, Mary Barnes, Alison Presdee, Trish Bolter, Brian Daniels, Karl Davies, Shirley Davies, Ann Strange, Chris Davies, Doris Bailey, Linda Mathias, Iris Thomas, Joan Phipps, Maureen Jackson and Pat Briton.

Mrs Coggins' general store at the end of Vincent Avenue, Nantyglo. The original shop opened in 1936 in the small tin shed to the right. The large green building was formerly the cricket pavilion from Brynmawr Park. It was bought by Mrs Coggins in 1953 and served as a general store until 1988.

Gaynor Rowberry with Margaret and Les Mogford on the shop's very last day of business, 29 October 1988. Every adult customer received a free drink and each child a packet of sweets.

Four

Views around the Valley

Tom Godwin and family on the Garn Road in 1900. Tom was a boxing manager, haulage contractor and undertaker. The little girl on the left became Mrs Ashton. The girl on the right became Mrs Collins. She died recently at the age of 94. The family were so fond of their dog, Trump (centre) that when it died they had its head stuffed and mounted and hung it on the passage wall in the house!

Long Row, Nantyglo, built in 1793 by Harford the ironmaster for the workers at Nantyglo Ironworks.

New Road, Nantyglo in the days of horse-drawn transport. The miners' institute on the left was built in 1912.

Gilwern village, c.1900. The horse is standing next to an old iron drinking trough which occupied the spot for many years.

Stables and cottages at Nantyglo, owned in the nineteenth century by Crawshay Bailey, 1970s.

Hay-making near Nantyglo, c.1910, on the land where Vincent Avenue and the Ffosmaen estate (built 1921) now stands. The whitewashed building in the distance is the Ffosmaen Inn.

Trostre Farm, c.1910. The farm's arched doorways, iron-studded solid-oak door and tiny mullioned windows suggest that the farm dates back to medieval times. Before the industrial revolution drovers visited the farm to buy cattle. Local legend has it that on one occasion a drover returned to the farm where earlier that day he had purchased cattle and murdered the farmer in order to recover his money.

Coronation Street, Blaina, built in 1902 for workers of the John Lancaster Company.

New Road and police station, Nantyglo, *c.*1930. The road was built in 1892.

The bottom of Beaufort Street, Brynmawr, c.1910. The site of the small pub, the Old Castle Inn (proprietor W. Lewis) on the right is now covered by the Griffin Hotel. The women on the left can be seen carrying their children in a shawl, Welsh fashion.

Brynmawr Square, pre-1912, with, on the right, Morgan's Commercial Temperance Hotel, now the Homestead Cafe.

Blaina High Street, c.1910. The open area behind the wall on the right is now the site of the Blaina Rugby Club.

Glamorgan Street, Brynmawr, c.1900. On the right stands the King William IV pub and the Founder's pub. On the left is the Shoulder of Mutton. At one time there were no less than seven pubs in this one street alone.

Coalbrookvale after the flood of 1913. The old Ironworks' coke ovens can be seen just above the waterline.

Garn Road, c.1920. The houses here were built in the 1830s for workers at the Nantyglo Ironworks. On the extreme right is the old Hector Inn, now the site of a bungalow.

Bayliss Row, built by Crawshay Bailey in 1826 for his workers. Because they overlooked Tŷ Mawr, his mansion, they were built without any windows on that side so that the ironmaster's "privacy" would be maintained. Windows did not begin to be added until after Bailey's death in 1872.

Mrs Sullivan outside the clod house on the Nantyglo side of the Blaenafon road, 1929. Similar houses had been used as first-stage accomodation for workers coming into the area in the early part of the nineteenth century, particularly by the pit sinkers who arrived from the Somerset coalfield.

Left: Mr Harry Godwin pictured after successfully coursing hare, 1920. The area in the background is now covered by Gwent Terrace.

Below: Nantyglo post office, King Street, 1920s, with a daughter of Mrs Morgan the postmistress and assistant on the front step. A post office was first recorded at that address in 1871.

Children sledging down the Red Hill, Market Road, Nantyglo in 1926. Left hand sledge: Harry Evans, Ron Phillips, -?-, Josh Hathaway, -?-, Ron Boulter, Cyril Holland. Right sledge: -?-, -?-, -?-, Ray Williams, Arthur Watkins, Bill James, E. Hathaway, Ron Davies, Jackie Stokes, Bill Evans. Watching: -?-, -?-, -?-, -?-, Marie Arnold, R. Parry, Dai Parry, Noel Watts, -?-, Len Clark, Stan Davies, T. Nash.

Gypsy encampment among the Brynmawr coal tips, 1928.

Nantyglo and Blaina Urban District Council refuse cart, 1929. The driver was David Edwards, known locally as "Dai Dusty" on account of his job.

Unemployed men at the Square, Brynmawr on a rainy day in 1931. Reputed to have been in attendance was William Joyce (a.k.a. Lord Haw-Haw) who broadcast German propaganda on the wireless during the Second World War. He was at Brynmawr for a short time as a member of the International Students Movement which was involved in the building of the swimming pool in the town. In one of his wartime tirades against the British system he was to mention the scene shown in this photograph: "You men standing on the corner in the rain in Brynmawr..."

A Griffin bus passes through Queen Street, Nantyglo during the great storm of 1934. The large building in the background is the Royal Oak Inn, formerly the home of the Chartist leader, Zephaniah Williams.

A pedigree dog belonging to Mr Parry, 1930s. In the backgound, on the right, can be seen Long Row and the crushing plant.

Bailey Street, Brynmawr, formerly the route of Crawshay Bailey's tramroad to Llangattock.

King Street and Garn Road, 1937. Notice the unemployed men whiling away their time on the street corner. The large house in the centre is called Mount Pleasant and was built about 1830.

Bringing in the coal, Shinton's Row, West Side, Blaina.

A wartime view of Croes-y-Ceiliog, Nantyglo. The area is now covered by the car park for the Beacon View flats.

The Waun Pond as it was before the construction of the Dunlop Semtex Factory. It was originally used as a source of water for the Nantyglo Ironworks.

Garn Cross, 1930s. On the left is Williams' chemist's above which were the Victoria Rooms. It was here that the first meeting of the district education board took place in 1875. Visible on the right is the Vine Inn.

Above: Lower High Street, Blaina, 1946. The large building in the background, now the Blaina Workmen's Club, was formerly the Castle Inn.

Right: Mrs Ann Hancock of Chapel Farm delivering milk to Coalbrookvale in 1948.

Black Rank – split-level workers' housing built in the 1820s, viewed here in the 1940s during the construction of the pre-fab buildings which were to develop into the Glanystruth housing estate.

Blaina Square and Institute, 1954.

View from Brynmawr towards Nantyglo, 1951. To the right the building of the Waun Ebbw houses is underway. Beyond the Waun Pond is the original reservoir built to supply the Nantyglo Ironworks in 1795.

Brynmawr Square, 1950s. In the background can be seen the Market Hall which has recently celebrated its centenary.

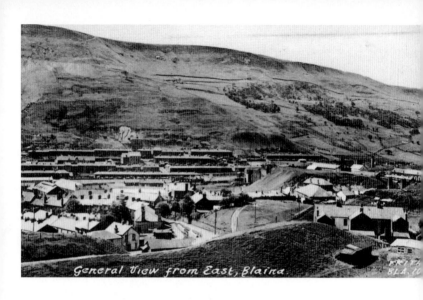

Above: View of Blaina, 1950s.

Left: Little Judith Bunn with Megan Morgan on Garn Road in 1962. All the houses in the background have since been demolished and the whole area is now landscaped.

Above: Snowdrifts near Lion Row, Nantyglo, January 1963.

Right: Tŷ Bryn Maen in the valley above Cwm Celyn. A fine example of a Welsh long-house it has a date stone inscribed 1693. Translated from the Welsh the farm's name means "house on the hill of the stone" and this refers to a nearby Bronze-Age standing stone.

Mr Malcolm Hancock shearing sheep at Chapel Farm in the 1970s.

Chapel Farm, 1970s. This is a good example of a cruck-built farmhouse of the fifteenth century, a cruck being a curved timber. It dates back to 1474 and has an oak-frame supporting a steeply-pitched roof which would originally have been covered with stone tiles. The house belongs to Malcolm and Betty Hancock and is still a working farm. It has been in the Hancock family since 1933.

Five

Serving the Community

Brynmawr St John's ambulance brigade outside the Market Hall in the 1920s.

Unemployed men undertaking voluntary work organised by the Quakers at Brynmawr in 1928.

Brynmawr swimming pool nearing completion in 1930. This project was also organised by the Quakers. In the centre of the picture, wearing the light-coloured plus-fours, is Lord Jim Forrester – a leading Quaker.

Workmen pictured on the railway line to Beynon's Colliery near the old youth club on West Side. Railway Terrace is in the background.

The Drums and Bugles of 275 Squadron (Nantyglo) of the Air Training Corps (A.T.C.), 1942-43. Among those pictured are Jackie Barrett, John Weekes, Des Thomas, Billy Watkins, Islwyn Tucker, Emlyn Johns and Fred Griffiths.

Members of the Nantyglo Ex-Servicemen's Club, 1950s.

Mr Fred Griffiths (headmaster of Garnfach School) receiving his O.B.E. at Buckingham Palace in 1962. On the left is Mrs Nellie Griffiths and to the right, Lilian Evans, headmistress of Winchestown School.

Alexander Cordell presenting Trevor Rowson with a carved walking stick in 1985. From left to right: Sheila Rowson, Pat Ellis, Trevor Rowson, Alexander Cordell, Donnie Cordell, John Ellis, Aubrey Barnes.

Cllr Eric Gwillym, Mayor of Nantyglo and Blaina being interviewed by the B.B.C. at the closure of Nantyglo School on 17 July 1991. Dr Nookaraju is on the right of the picture. Many people had travelled considerable distances to attend this sad event, including some evacuees who had attended the school during the Second World War.

Six

Education

Staff at Blaina Central School, 1911. The headmistress was Ellen Athay.

Nantyglo Central School, 1912. The headmaster was William Roberts. There is a stark difference between school photographs taken in the early years of this century and those of the late 1920s and 1930s where, despite the best efforts of the parents struggling to keep homes together during the Depression, the children are generally poorly dressed with a malnourished air.

Blaina Central School, *c.*1920. The school was opened in 1884 and was extended between 1906 and 1908. It had capacity for 407 boys, 407 girls and 406 infants.

Class 2 at Winchestown Mixed Junior School, 1920.

Garnfach Infants class IIb, 1922.

Nantyglo and Blaina boys on camp at Ogmore, late 1930s. Among those pictured are Aubrey Barnes, Ted Evans, Billy Watkins and Bill Rowson.

Nantyglo and Blaina girls in camp in the 1930s. Visible in the picture are Nancy Hardwick, Jean King, Joan Vaughan, Doris Pugh, Ivy Fisher, Hilda Jones, Miss Beardmore and Miriam Morgan.

Garnfach School with headmaster Archie Hughes (centre). Among those pictured are Maureen Madden, Ian Maidment, Terry Gray, John Flemings and the Harper twins, Graham and Gerald.

Glan-yr-afon Secondary Modern School Form IX (Boys), 1957 with their form master, Mr Silk. Back row: D. Baton, Martin Lewis, John Collins, Michael Staley, Ralph Coburn, Dennis Vaughan, Barry George, Lyndon Briton, John Coles, Lionel Hillman. Middle row: Gary Smith, Graham Hill, Brian Legge, Alan Jones, Jerry Silk, Arthur Poulson, Fred Wellington, Michael Griffith, Dennis Gunter, David Williams, David O'Brien, Granville Isaacs. Front row: Graham Nash, Clive Jones, Gerald Heaton, Brian Bevan, Martin Davies, Marrie Madden, Martin Perry, Malcolm MacDonald, John Brookes, David Cayford, Brian Mann, Rawdon Morris.

Blaina West Side School, 1960.

Blaina Infants School, May 1960. Back row: David Jones, Gerald Williams, Melvin Barrett, Keith Hillman, Leighton Davies, Gary Knapp, Stephen Roberts, Mike Ayres, Kevin Williams, Stephen Ruddock, Brian Matthews, Martin Parfitt, -?-, Stephen Trapnell, Gareth Griffiths, George Withey.

Garnfach School Christmas Party, 1956. Those pictured include Kay Fear, Kay Lewis, Megan Steel, Gwyneth Harris, Ann Williams, Dawn Nash, Rawdon Morris, Lyn Watkins, Graham Hall, Janice Grey.

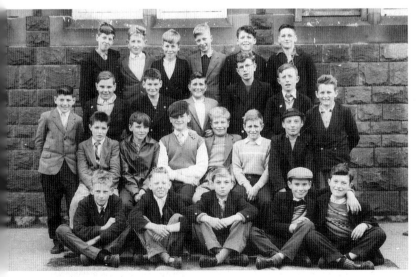

Glan-yr-afon School, 1957.

Garnfach School, 1960. From left to right, back row: Carol Oldham, Maureen Barker, Mair Saunders, Yvonne Mogford, Margaret Turner, Carol Hughes, Pat Vaughan, Denise Wheeler, Christine Broderick. Middle row: Lorraine Prisk, Barry Curtis, John Lewis, Richard Johns, John Bevington, Rusell Davies, Denzil Wright, David Barrett, Harold Lloyd, Ken Williams, Malcolm Hawkins, Elaine Barnes. Front row: Elizabeth Bowen, Shirley Clarke, Gillian Griffiths, Ann Cooksey, Christine Hannan, Barbara Martin, ? Saunders, Susan Barker, Pam Barker. Seated on floor: Colin Nash, Michael Collins, Steven Hughes, David Fawkes, Carl Lewis.

Garnfach School kitchen staff, 1960s. Back row: E. Williams, M. Barnes, D. Evans. Bottom row: G. Curtis, F. Griffiths (headmaster), V. Knowles.

Staff at Nantyglo Junior School with Trevor Jenkins (headmaster) and Arthur Fawkes (caretaker).

Nantyglo Junior School, Class 5 with headmaster, Max Joynson and teacher, Mrs Watkins, 1980. From right to left, back row: Mark Jones, Byron Isaac, Jason Strange, Matthew Nelson, -?-. Third row: Lee Davies, Lisa Stead, Emma Bristow, Nicola Cole, Jane Thomas, Lee Lyndon Cole. Second row: Kathryn Oldham, Joanna Wright, Nicola Jones, Trudy Rogers, -?-, Terry Ann Davies, Mandy Holland. Front row: Darren Prewitt, Andrew Webley, Lee Bufton, Richard Bainton.

Mrs Eunice Sims, the last head teacher at Nantyglo Junior School which closed in 1991. She had been a teacher at the school for 25 years.

Nantyglo Junior School, 1991, prior to demolition.

Seven

Religion

Bethlehem Chapel, Clydach. This was opened in 1850 next to the Beaufort–Gilwern tramroad (built 1795).

St Peter's Whitsun walkers gathering on the square at Blaina, *c.*1910.

St Peter's Whitsun walk, Blaina Square, c.1908. Note the difference between this and the photograph on the last two pages. This view shows the Blaina Institute before it was rendered and the Red Lion before substantial reconstruction was undertaken.

Bethel Chapel Whitsun walk, 1930s.

St Ann's Church Sunday school walk, Nantyglo, 1929. Amongst the children walking are Arthur Carpenter, Jimmy Preece and Stanley Elliott (the first Blaina man to be killed during the Second World War).

Evan Gibbons – as a small child he fell off a wall and the lower part of his legs had to be amputated. Mr Hale, the local cobbler in Nantyglo, made Evan a special pair of shoes allowing him to walk on his knees. Every Whitsun, Evan, who lived in Coalbrook, would lead the school walks right around Nantyglo walking for several miles.

Men from Nantyglo and Blaina at a camp organised by the Quakers at Talgarth, Breconshire in 1934.

Whitsun walk by the Wesleyan Chapel, Nantyglo, 1950.

Nantyglo Church Band of Hope concert, 1930s.

The congregation of the Mission Church combined with that of St Peter's for the Whitsun walk of 1949. Among those pictured are Tony Williams, Mr Blundon, Mr Norster, Ken Hale, Mrs Jenkins, Miss Hippy, and Edith Poulson.

The two churches combined the following Whitsun for the 1950 walk. Some of those present are Keith Price, David Watkins, Mrs Bridges, Mrs Hughes (the rector's wife), Jean Norster, Mary Griffiths, Flora Lockstone, Sheila Millwall, Joan Harford, Nelly Hale, Olwen Evans, Margaret Powell, Mrs Jenkins, Muriel Wall, Iris Harford, Mrs Morgan.

Whitsun walk through Blaina.

Nantyglo Welsh Wesleyan Chapel's Whitsun walk along Limestone Road in 1957. Among those pictured are Mary Rees, Joan Cooksey, Marion Foote, Jean O'Brian, Joyce Daley, R. Lochlan, E. Lochlan, Mrs Jones.

Whitsun walk by Salem Chapel Sunday school, Winchestown, 1956.

A Whitsun walk passes the Greyhound in 1960. Among those pictured are Elaine Barnes and Nancy Williams.

Whitsun walk, 1960. Among the procession are Enid Nash, J. Vaughan, G. Porter and M. Barnes.

Holy Trinity Church, Nantyglo. The church was consecrated on 10 August 1854 and dedicated to the Holy Trinity. The patronage was vested in the Crown and the Bishop of Llandaff alternately.

Left: Ann Bevan and Hazel Thomas among the walkers at Whitsun, Nantyglo, 1961.

Below: Interior of the old St Peter's church, Blaina which was demolished in 1969 thereby removing the distinctive landmark at Blaina's heart.

Eight

Clubs, Entertainment and Holidays

Garnfach juvenile choir, c.1925. The conductor was Mr Tom Lewis and under him the choir enjoyed considerable success through South Wales.

Above: Mr Tom Lewis and family of Nantyglo, winners of over 1,000 eisteddfod prizes. On the extreme left is Master Tom Lewis ("the Wonder Boy Conductor") and on the far right is Mr Jack Lewis (finalist in the Gwilym Gwent Scholarship competition held at Nantyglo).

Left: Jack Lewis as he appeared at the Empire Theatre in Blaina in the 1920s. Other illustrious artistes who appeared at the old Empire included William "Buffalo Bill" Cody and Charlie Chaplin.

When Bostock & Womble's Menagarie visited Brynmawr in the 1920s the bear escaped and killed a young boy near Davies's photography shop. A Mr Ike Bartlett of Brynmawr, who was nearby, faced down the bear and killed it. An act of immense, if reckless, courage.

This photograph, and the others on these two pages, shows Blaina miners, their families and friends in the Herefordshire hopfields in the 1930s. Each summer there used to be an exodus of workers to the hopfields, a reference being made to this annual ritual as early as 1813 in Wood's *The Rivers of Wales*. Many miners took advantage of the work in the hopfields and considered it a holiday. Some would even fake illness in order to go and parents were sometimes taken to court because their children had gone hop-picking instead of attending school.

Hop-picking, 1930s.

Hop-picking, 1930s.

Hop-picking, 1940s. On the left of this picture can be seen Mr & Mrs Rowberry and Terence Rowberry of Nantyglo.

Building the Bannau Park in 1931 under the auspices of the Blue Pilgrims. The young boy second from the left in the front row is young Arthur Fear. In the background on the right hand side is the winding house on the old Rope Pit, one of Nantyglo's earliest collieries which had closed on the site just after the turn of the twentieth century.

Mr & Mrs Parfitt (and goat) at Central Park attending the Blaina Miners' fête in 1932.

The Good Neighbours Club, set up in the 1930s for the unemployed – they would repair boots and organise games of dominoes and skittles. In the middle of the picture in the muffler and flat cap is Dick Martin and to his left can be seen Mr Williams (moustache) and Fred Pugh (glasses and striped scarf). To Mr Martins's left, in the waistcoat and glasses, is William Davies "Codi-moch" (pig-keeper).

Above: Blaina accordion band, 1930s. Among those pictured are Jim Jones and John Gardner.

Left: Dr Carlin crowning the Blaina Carnival Queen, 1930s. This doctor was held in such high esteem by the local community that Carlin Road on the Coedcae was named after him.

Street party held in King Street, Nantyglo to celebrate the coronation of George VI in 1937.

Nantyglo Church outing to Porthcawl in the 1930s. From left to right: J. Sims, D. Sims, Mrs Sims, John Taylor, Trevor Taylor, George Taylor, Mrs Taylor, Marjorie Lloyd, Mrs Lloyd, Marjorie Pritchard, Mrs Pritchard, Mrs Bevan, Mrs Harris, Evan Gibbons, Mrs Wedgbury, Vernon Treharne, Tommy Jones, Mrs Prior, Violet Pritchard.

Above: V.E. Day celebrations, Maes Hafod, Blaina, 1945.

Left: A V.E. Day street party in Bryn Hyfryd, Nantyglo, 1945. Among those pictured are Ivy Jones, Don Phillips, Ronnie Treherne, Glyn Davies, John Davies, Graham and Gerald Harper, Nora Whittaker, Carol Jones, Marilyn Jenkins. The soldier in uniform is Bert Harper.

Blaina pensioners' outing, c.1950. Notice the gas-holder in the background.

Bridgend Inn and the Brecon and Monmouthshire Canal at Gilwern in the 1940s. After the virtual cessation in the use of canals for industrial and commercial transport purposes they gained a second lease of life as a leisure facility.

A fancy-dress entry in the Blaina Carnival which co-incided in 1951 with nationwide celebrations for the Festival of Britain.

Blaina Carnival, 1951. The adults pictured are G. Hancocks, M. Hancocks, G. Derrick, S. Derrick and the children are: Anne Hancocks, Lynne Watkins, Andrew Derrick, Diana Derrick.

Nantyglo Carnival, 1953, held as part of the celebrations for the coronation of Queen Elizabeth II. The bride and groom at the head of the procession are Mrs Huggins and her daughter-in-law, Edna Huggins.

Women from West Side, Blaina on a trip to Blackpool in 1953. Among those pictured are Nell Rees, Bess Gardner, Mrs Giles, Mrs Hale, Gwen Gardner, Audrey Beecham, Doll Rees, Gwen Rees, Mrs Wakely, Mrs Maidment, Mrs Morgan.

Chivers' coach trip to Porthcawl in 1957. Second from the left is Sid Swithin (driver) with his daughter, Jeanette and his wife, Anne.

Nantyglo Hit Paraders concert party in the 1950s. From left to right: Gwyn Nash (pianist), Billy "Bronco" Williams, Alf Davis, Don Richards, John Bailey, Mr James, Rees Dimmick, Denis Tibbs, Jack Williams, Ron Rees, Tom Tibbs with Bryn Lovett (seated).

Blaina pensioners' Christmas party. In the picture can be seen I. Lloyd Jones, John Dimmick (Queen Street), David Davies (Abertillery Road), Fred Price, William Clayton (Lancaster Street, William Austin (West Side), Albert Lane (West Side), David Jenkins, J. Herbert (Church Street) and Mr Williams (Coronation Street).

Nantyglo Workmen's Club ladies Christmas dinner, 1960s. From left to right, back row: Eliza Jones, -?-, Norma Swanson, Lily Williams, Mary Clarke, Matilda Besant, Phyllis Purse, Eira Tibbs, Olive Broderick, Kate Whitby, Millie Best. Middle row: Beatrice Titford, Jackie Cooper, Gwen Roberts, Florrie Edwards, Vashti Roberts, Gladys Jenkins, Susan Bowers, Doreen Williams. Font row: Angela Cooper, Carol Price, Lillian Nash, Mrs Morgan, Kath Williamson, Margorie Price.

Brynhyfryd Avenue's street party to celebrate the Investiture of Prince Charles as Prince of Wales in 1969. Among those pictured are Mrs Barnes, Mrs Johnson, Nora Whittaker, Etta Silcox and Ethel Rowson.

Janice Davies guides the Prince of Wales through the excavation work at Tŷ Mawr (Crawshay Bailey's residence in the nineteenth century), 1981.

Blaina "21" Club in the 1960s. Their meetings were held once a month at the Old Hafodians Club. From left to right, back row: -?-, George Lewis, Dennis Herrington, Graham Best, Albert Brown, Mr Thompson. Middle row: -?-, Norman Bayton, Rumsy James, Jack Morris, Mr Thompson, Dick Bennett. Front row: Islwyn Huggins, Eddie Jones, Fred Hopkins, Eddie Furber, Fred Marshman.

A "knobbly-knees" competition held at the Nantyglo Workingmen's Club in the 1970s. The winner was Dai Wilkins and the runner-up, John Payne. Among the others pictured are Jack Britton, Ernie Probert and Mostyn Thomas.

The Bow-tie Club Christmas Party held in the Nantyglo Workingmen's Club in 1973.

The Bow-tie Club that same Christmas 1973. From right to left, back row: Jack Elkins, David Broderick, Bill Cooper, Wilf John, David Wilkins, Gordon Purse, Roy Edmunds, Graham Morgan, Alan Cole, Harry Richards, Jack Nash. Middle row: Wilf Morgan, John Mogford, David George, Alan Price, Gerald Teague, Joe Havard, Albert Nash, Ronnie Rees, Howard Fawkes, Ray Robinson. Seated: Gabe Barnes, Ken Jenkins, Jim Lewis, Bill Mogford.

Nine

Sport

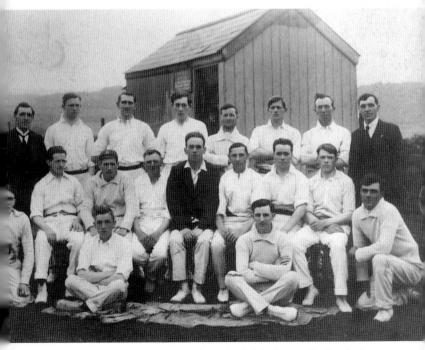

Waen Marsley cricket team, 1910. They played on a levelled slag heap at Coalbrookvale.

Nantyglo snooker team, winners of the South Wales Challenge Shield in the 1930s. Among those pictured are Bert Lowry, Con Cave, Walter Davies, Howey Fawke, Haydn Jones and Bryn Jones.

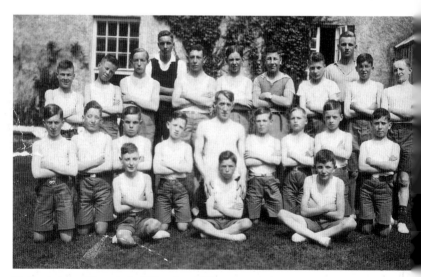

The newly-formed Nantyglo Boys' Brigade, c. 1933.

Duffryn Park, Blaina, built by unemployed men in 1928.

Bannau Park tennis courts in the 1940s. To the right can be seen Cwm Crachen and the slag heaps produced by the Nantyglo Ironworks through the nineteenth century.

General View of the Lido, Brynmawr. 1087.

Brynmawr Lido, built by unemployed workers in the 1930s, under the direction of the Quakers.

The Brynmawr Lido being put to enthusiastic use by local people, 1930s.

275 A.T.C. Squadron "B" rugby XV, 1942-43. Among those pictured are I. Rogers, N. Thomas, E. Watkins, F. Griffiths, I. Roberts, B. Smith, D. Horton, B. Vaughan, E. Clark, E. Evans, N. Williamson, G. Watkins and D. Jones.

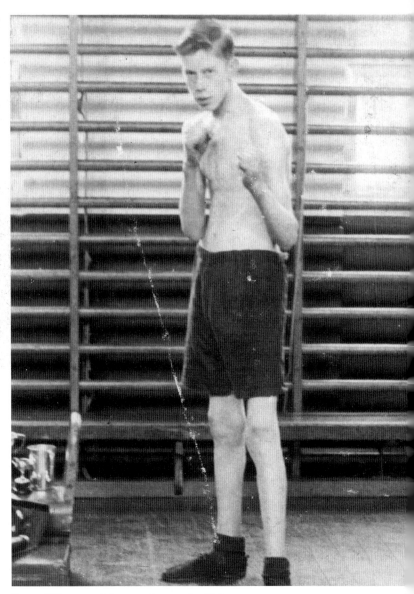

Tommy Tibbs, successful amateur boxer in the 1940s.

Blaina R.F.C., 1946-47 season. This team lost to Brynmawr in the local cup final by a penalty goal. From left to right, back row: R. Norster, E.J. Davies, R. Hathaway, L. Griffin, W. Harris, E.G. Hiscox, R. Williams (trainer). Middle row: I. Phillips, H. Norster, R. Davies, W. Smith, D. Herrington. Front row: M. Knapp, M. Jones, A. Jackson, M. Thomas.

Winchestown cricket team playing at Penarth in 1951. From left to right, back row: Keith Stone, Emrys Porter, Cliff Ford, Trevor Harty, Bill Porter, Donald Palmer. Middle row: Cliff Clark, Tom Rees, Wally Price, David Ford, Jack George, Arthur Ford. Front row: William John Stone, Maldwyn Beynon, Tom Ford.

The undefeated Glan-yr-Afon Secondary Modern School rugby XV, 1954-55 season. From left to right, back row: L. Morgan (headmaster), L. Jones, C. Gore, L. Hathaway, D. Watkins, M. Cayford, J. Davies, J. James, R. James. Middle row: R. Wilkins, D. Griffiths, E. Davies (captain), C. Sanders, R. Stevens. Front row: B. Daniels, H. Holmes, G. Smith, J. Cole.

Mr John Sims of Nantyglo, an outstanding motor-cyclist and member of the Beaufort Cycling Club, passes through Beaufort in a motor-cycle rally in the 1950s.

Nantyglo football team, 1954-55 season. Among those pictured are Don Phillips, Ken Titford, Monty Lewis, Granville Brown, Derek Tucker, Keith Davies, Cllr Jack Durban and Bryn Hurll.

Cwm Celyn R.F.C., 1959, winners of the Monmouthshire Youth Cup. From left to right, back row: R. Hill, J. Watkins, G. Jones, R. Pointing, A. Silk, R. Tilling, M. Dixon, J. Hill, A. Evans, R. Overton, R. Cayford. Middle row: R. James, M. Cayford, -?-, C. Morgan, A. Davies, -?-, D. Hawkins, I. Jones. Front row: G. Edwards, D. Watkins, R. Wall.

Cwm Celyn Youth rugby team, 1959, winners of the Abertillery Junior Sevens. From left to right, back row: R. James, A. Evans, R. Pointing, R. Hill, R. Tillings, M. Dixon, R. Cayford. Middle row: J. Watkins, R. Overton, -?-, I. Jones. Font row: C. Morgan, D. Watkins, M. Cayford.

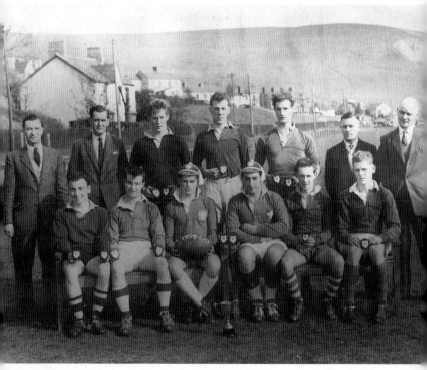

Cwm Celyn Youth rugby team, 1960, winners of the Monmouthshire Youth Sevens tournament. From left to right, back row: I.Jones, R. James, A. Evans, J. Evans, M. Dixon, J. Watkins, R. Cayford. Front row: A. Bull, M. Cayford, D. Watkins, D. Paul, G. Phillips.

Opposite above: Nantyglo All Blacks R.F.C., 1938. The players were Stan Edwards, Gwilym Edwards, "Crash" Harding, Jasper James, Vernon Thomas, Alwyn Barnes, "Dinkey" Cooksey, Billy Barnes, Jim Jeffries, Joe Purnell, Glyn Griffiths, "Browdo" Thomas, Billy Edwards, Harold Edwards, Alf Player, Emlyn Tudgey.

Opposite below: Llanelly Hill football team, *c.* 1963. From left to right, back row: M. Watts, T. Alexandra, T. Johns, J. Brooks, M. Williams (goalkeeper), O. Jones. Front row: D. Walters, D. Thomas, J. Welsh, M. Jones, R. Bratt, M. Jones, J. Perret, G. Luff.

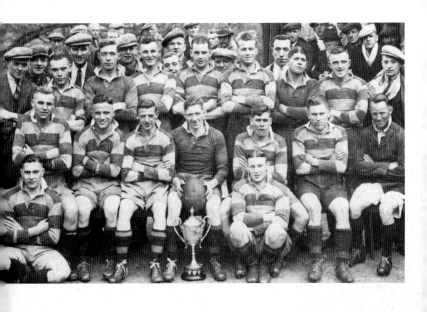

Michael Elliott in 1962 when he was still playing for Cwm Celyn Youth. He was soon to be signed by Oldham to play rugby league.

Ebbw Vale and District under-21s team which faced the Wellington tourists from New Zealand, 21 November 1984. From right to left, back row: Chris Walmesley, Paul Stewart (Brynmawr), Wayne Matthews, Paul Wedgebury (Brynmawr), Huw Evans, Steve Lewis, Carl Grey, Darren Hughes (Brynmawr), Glen Williams, David Evans, Mike Davies, David Powell. Front row: Andrew Welsh, Huw Jones, Mike Jones, Ian Watkins (captain from Ebbw Vale), Andrew Morgan, Jeff Lapham, Chris Sculley. Kneeling: Steve Fealey, Steve Jones (Brynmawr).

Ten-year-old Dawson Morris receiving his prize from the Mayor of Nantyglo and Blaina, Cllr Billy Wheeler, at the County sports held at Blaina in 1986.

Acknowledgements

I am indebted to the following local people whose assistance in the gathering of material for this book has been invaluable. The inclusion of their photographs has enabled the compilation of a richer and more comprehensive collection and together we have been able to unearth some real treasures. A. Barnes, Don Bearcroft (Curator of Abertillery and District Museum), M. Beynon, M. Cayford, Mr Chaffey, J. Cox, M. Hancock, C. Harris, E. Huggins, D. Jones, N. Lewis, G. Morris, G. Nash, A. Pugh, T. Rowberry, E. Sims, J. Sims, G. Taylor, G. Thomas, I. Thomas, D.C. Whittaker.

I would also like to thank Mr Frank Olding, Curator at Abergavenny Castle Museum not only for supplying an excellent foreword but also for his advice and assistance during the preparation of the book.

Finally, I would like to thank those people who offered material which due to pressures of space I was sadly not able to include and to apologise to anyone who may have contributed and has not been mentioned in these acknowledgements. To everyone who has turned the pages this far I very much hope that you have enjoyed what you have read and seen, and that many memories of our past have been evoked.

One of Crawshay Bailey's fortified roundhouses picured here in the early 1970s before their restoration.